MW01599615

Discovering Your P.U.R.P.O.S.E.

Volume One:
Primary Passions,
Underlying Values
and Mission Statement

David R. Hibbert

Destiny Media Productions
Brossard, Quebec, Canada

Discovering Your P.U.R.P.O.S.E.
Volume One: Primary Passions, Underlying Values and Mission Statement
© 2011, 2017 by David R. Hibbert

Destiny Media Productions
P.O. Box 30504
Brossard, Quebec, Canada J4Z 3R6
(450) 676-6944
Email: resource@destinyresource.ca
Website: www.destinyresource.ca

ISBN Paperback: 978-1-988738-18-5
ISBN Digital Book: ISBN 978-1-988738-19-2

Cover design by Melissa Baker-Nguyen of Lost Bumblebee Graphics. Address inquiries to lostbumblebee@gmail.com

Table Of Contents

Introduction

You have a purpose, a destiny, a special assignment from God Himself! And when you discover that purpose, commit to that purpose, and make decisions in alignment with that purpose, the Creator of the universe ensures that all of the resources in heaven and earth are directed toward you, so that you can fulfill that purpose.

There are seven primary indicators that God has given you, to help you discover what is your purpose in life.

In **Volume One** of "Discovering Your P.U.R.P.O.S.E.", you will be taught the first two indicators to discover what is your purpose, and then be guided, step by step, to developing your own personal Mission Statement for your life, that you can use to help you stay on track, and make the best decisions for your life's purpose.

In **Volume Two** of "Discovering Your P.U.R.P.O.S.E.", you will be taught the last five indicators to discover what is your purpose, and then be guided, step by step, to evaluate all seven indicators, put them together into a personal profile, and develop a personal plan for your life, so that you can fulfill your life's purpose.

Section 1 – You Have A Purpose!

Your Goal:

To discover that there is an answer to the
question,
"Why Am I Here?"
and to realize that you have a mission in life.

Living In The Dash

I read of a man who stood to speak
At the funeral of a friend.
He referred to the dates on her tombstone
From the beginning…. to the end.
He noted that first came her date of birth
And spoke the following date with tears,
But he said what mattered most of all
Was the dash between those years. (1900 - 1970)

For that dash represents all the time
That she spent alive on earth.
And now only those who loved her
Know what that little line is worth.
For it matters not, how much we own;
The cars…. the house…. the cash,
What matters is how we live and love
And how we spend our dash.

So think about this long and hard….
Are there things you'd like to change?
For you never know how much time is left,
That can still be rearranged.
If we could just slow down enough
To consider what's true and real,
And always try to understand
The way other people feel.

And be less quick to anger,
And show appreciation more
And love the people in our lives
Like we've never loved before.
If we treat each other with respect,
And more often wear a smile.
Remembering that this special dash
Might only last a little while.

So, when your eulogy's being read
With your life's actions to rehash....
Would you be proud of the things they say
About how you spent your dash?

The Dash Poem[1]
© 1996 Linda Ellis
http://lindaellis.net/

God's Plans - Our Choices

God's Word To You:
"For I know the plans I have for you", declares the Lord,
"Plans to prosper you and not to harm you,
plans to give you hope and a future."
Jeremiah 29:11, NIV

Your Desired Word to God:
"I have fought the good fight, I have finished the race,
I have kept the faith."
2 Timothy 4:7, NIV

God's Conditional Final Word to You:
"Well done, good and faithful servant! You have been faithful with
a few things;
I will put you in charge of many things.
Come and share your Master's happiness."
Matthew 25:21, NIV

Are You On The Right Path?

The average person makes 35,000 remotely conscious decisions a day, including 226.7 decisions on food alone.[2] Each decision we make takes us either closer to, or further from our purpose in life. Do you know where you are going? How do you know which path to take?

There was a sign on the Alaska-Canada (Alcan) highway at the Alaska border in the 1960s that said "Choose your rut carefully – you will be in it for the next 200 miles."[3]

Each person has a unique, God-given path to follow in their lives, in order to fulfill their destiny. By our choices, we choose whether that path is a rut to control us, or a road to guide us.

A rut is a path that keeps us trapped, and often takes us where we don't want to go. A road is a path that guides us each day, but gives us the freedom to steer and turn as needed, so that we can get to where we need to go.

So....

- Are you on the right path?
- How do you know if you are on the right path?
- Do you need to change paths?
- Do you know how to change paths?
- Do you know what path to choose?
- How will you determine what path to choose?

Thomas Merton said that the greatest tragedy in life is to climb the ladder of success, and find out at the end of your life, that your ladder was leaning against the wrong wall.[4]

Our quest for the right path should begin with some very difficult, but revealing questions:

- Am I presently doing what I feel is the most important thing for my life?
- Am I presently doing what brings me the most satisfaction and fulfillment in my life?
- Am I presently doing what will affect my life positively, 20 years from now?
- Am I presently doing through my lifestyle and actions, what reflects what I really believe?
- Am I presently doing what keeps me motivated?
- Am I presently doing what allows me to leave a good legacy for others?
- Am I presently doing what I would still be doing, even if I only had one year left to live?
- Am I presently doing what captures my heart?
- Am I presently doing what brings me the greatest joy?
- Am I presently doing what I am willing to be known for, by others?

Through these two workbooks, you are going to be given the tools you need to discover what your purpose in life is, what path you need to be on, and how to get to where you need to go. That's what "Purpose" is all about. Purpose is not just knowing what you should be doing, but also being able to "picture" what you should be doing, knowing what steps to take to get there, and being able to monitor your progress to make sure that you stay on track.

Initial Discovery Questions

If you knew that you would not fail, what would you set out to do with your life?

If you knew that you had unlimited financial resources, what big goals would you be setting?

If you knew that you had twenty years to build something for God, what exciting dream would you start building?

If you knew God would give you the wisdom and power to solve every problem, what challenging task would you undertake?

If you knew that you were at the end of your life preparing to stand before God, what would you wish you had done with your life?

If you knew that you had received ideas that were inspired by God Himself, which of those ideas have come to you that you have not acted upon?

If you knew that Jesus Christ was coming to you to take over the planning of your life, what goals would He be setting for your life?

If you knew that you only had one choice left in life, what cause do you believe is a cause worth dying for?

If you knew that God was promising you unlimited resources for a single goal in life, what great thing would you do for God before you die?

What thoughts of accomplishment come to you when you feel that you are the closest to God?

What thoughts of accomplishment come to you persistently and won't leave?

What thoughts of accomplishment bring you great joy and cause your heart to beat faster?

What things in life make you angry, grieves or disturbs you most?

What human needs, hurts or problems move you the deepest, and what solutions would you apply to these problems?

Whose life and accomplishments have inspired the deepest parts of your heart?

If you keep going in the direction you are headed right now, will you get where you want to go?

If you get to where you want to go, will you be happy and fulfilled at the deepest level of your heart?

Have other people encouraged you to stay on the path on which you are presently? Why or why not?

You Were Created For A Unique Purpose

2 Corinthians 5:5, NIV – *Now it is <u>God</u> who has <u>made us for</u> this very <u>purpose</u> and has given us the Spirit as a deposit, guaranteeing what is to come.*

Even before we were born, God had a special plan for each one of us, and so He created us with that plan in mind. When we give our lives to Him, He activates the fullness of that plan in us through the Holy Spirit. However, even before our salvation, that purpose was stirring in our hearts. So even before we committed our lives to Jesus Christ, we were motivated by God's purpose within us, but because we didn't have the Holy Spirit in our lives, our motives and actions were influenced by this world's perspective and value system.

Jeremiah 29:11, NIV – *"For I know the <u>plans</u> I have for you,"* declares the LORD, *"<u>plans</u> to prosper you and not to harm you, <u>plans</u> to give you hope and a <u>future</u>."*

Throughout our lives, God keeps His plans for our future in mind, and so every time we work in harmony with His plans for us, He adds His blessing to our activities. As a consequence, even when those who do not know Him serve His purpose for them, God will prosper them in that area of life.

I Have A Destiny

Early in my Christian life I heard this song, and it resonated with my spirit (and my heart). The truths in this song have been a constant reminder, and a constant encouragement to me over the years, and so I consider it to be one of my theme songs. I hope that its words may resonate in your heart also.

I Have A Destiny
by Mark Altrogge

(Chorus)

I have a destiny I know I shall fulfil
I have a destiny in that city on a hill[5]
I have a destiny and it's not an empty wish
For I know I was born for such a time as this[6]

(Verse 1)

Long before the ages You predestined me[7]
To walk in all the works You have prepared for me[8]
You've given me a part to play in history
To help prepare a bride for eternity[9]

(Verse 2)

I did not choose You but You have chosen me[10]
And appointed me for bearing fruit abundantly[11]
I know You will complete the work begun in me[12]
By the power of Your Spirit working mightily[13]

Click here for an arrangement performed by Bethel Praise[14]
Click here for an arrangement performed by Kent Henry[15]

How God Works With Us

1. God Works IN Us to Fulfill Our Purpose

Philippians 2:13, NIV — *"For it is God who works in you to will and to act according to his good purpose."*

God loves us so much, that He even works in our hearts by His Spirit to create in us the desire and willingness to act out His good purpose for us, so that He can bless us.

2. God Works FOR Us to Fulfill Our Purpose

Romans 8:28, NIV - *And we know that in all things God works for the good of those who love him, who have been called according to his purpose.*

Once we start to act out His good purpose in our lives, God brings "all things" ... all of the resources of heaven, to bear on our lives to ensure that we will succeed.

3. God Works AHEAD Of Us to Fulfill Our Purpose

Ephesians 2:10, NIV — *For we are God's workmanship, created in Christ Jesus to do good works, which God prepared in advance for us to do.*

God is so committed to helping us fulfill our purpose that He actually creates opportunities in advance for us to accomplish, so that we are more likely to stay on the pathway to our purpose.

4. God Works BEHIND Us to Fulfill Our Purpose

Jeremiah 15:11, NIV - *The LORD said, "Surely I will deliver you for a good purpose in times of disaster and times of distress."*

When we do face challenges or obstacles, or "mess up", God will intervene in our lives with the intention of freeing us out of those messes and helping us with the consequences of those messes, so that we can get back on track for our purpose.

5. **God Works <u>THROUGH</u> Us to Fulfill Our Purpose**

2 Thessalonians 1:11, NIV – *"With this in mind, we constantly pray for you, that <u>our God may</u> ... by his power ... <u>fulfill every good purpose of yours</u> and every act prompted by your faith."*

When our purpose is aligned with God's purpose, God works with us and through us, to ensure that His (and therefore our) purpose is fulfilled.

6. **God Works <u>WITH</u> Us to Fulfill Our Purpose**

Ephesians 1:11, NIV - *"In him we were also chosen, having been predestined according to the <u>plan</u> of him who <u>works out everything in conformity with the purpose of his will</u>."*

When we walk according to God's purpose for our lives, God will bring all sorts of other circumstances and external situations to bear on our lives, to help us fulfill His purpose for our lives.

Men and Women Who Fulfilled God's Purpose

Throughout the ages, great men and women have fulfilled God's purpose for their lives.

1. The Reign of Pharaoh

Exodus 9:16, NIV - *But I have raised you up for this very purpose, that I might show you my power and that my name might be proclaimed in all the earth.*

Even though Pharaoh did not know it, God even raised him up -- a pagan king -- because He had a specific purpose for him.

2. Children of Reuben, Gad and Manasseh

Joshua 22:3, NIV - *For a long time now -- to this very day -- you have not deserted your brothers but have carried out the mission the LORD your God gave you.*

God has a special mission or purpose for the children of Reuben, Gad and Manasseh, and He worked with them to ensure that they would fulfill it.

3. King David

Psalm 57:2, NIV - *I cry out to God Most High, to God, who fulfills his purpose for me.*

There was no doubt in King David's mind. God had raised him up to fulfill a very special purpose for the people of Israel.

4. Jesus

Isaiah 48:15, NIV – *I, even I, have spoken; yes, I have called him. I will bring him, and he will succeed in his mission.*

Acts 2:23 NIV - *This man was handed over to you by <u>God's set purpose</u> and foreknowledge; and you, with the help of wicked men, put him to death by nailing him to the cross.*

Jesus had a mission, a set purpose for coming to earth. Isaiah declared that He would succeed in His mission, and Peter proclaimed that God even used wicked men to ensure that Jesus would fulfill His purpose.

5. **Barnabas & Saul (Paul)**

    Acts 12:25, NIV - *When <u>Barnabas and Saul had finished their mission</u>, they returned from Jerusalem, taking with them John, also called Mark.*

    In Acts 11, Barnabas and Saul were commissioned by the church in Antioch to send a financial gift to the church in Judea. Even though King Herod had arrested a number of disciples in Jerusalem, including James the brother of John and Peter, Barnabas and Saul stayed in Jerusalem until they were sure that their "mission" was fulfilled.

    These are just some of the many examples of how God works with us, to fulfill His purpose, His mission for our lives.

What Will We Choose?

We all have a choice to either discover and embrace God's purpose for our lives, or to live for ourselves, and miss out on our destiny in Christ.

1. **Am I Willing to Discover, Embrace and Cooperate with God's Purpose for My Life?**

   Ephesians 2:10, NIV — *For we are God's workmanship, created in Christ Jesus to do good works, which God prepared in advance for us to do.*

   God created us for a purpose, and then prepared in advance good works for us to accomplish for Him. But will we choose to do them?

2. **Am I Willing to Reject God's Purpose and Miss Out On My Destiny?**

   Luke 7:30, NIV - *But the Pharisees and experts in the law rejected God's purpose for themselves....*

   The Pharisees and experts of the law rejected God's purpose for them. And they completely missed God's incredible plan for their lives.

3. **Am I Prepared To Come To the End of My Life and Stand Before God and Have to Make a Tragic Confession**

   Isaiah 49:4, NIV - *"... I have labored to no purpose. I have spent my strength in vain and for nothing. ..."*

   What a statement! I have indeed laboured, but I have laboured to no purpose. My work and sacrifice and struggle were pointless because I did not embrace God's purpose for my life.

4. Do I Desire To Come To The End Of My Life, And Have God Make A Good Declaration Over Me?

Acts 13:36, NIV - *For when <u>David had served God's purpose in his own generation</u>, he fell asleep ...*

David didn't try to convince people that He had accomplished God's purpose for His life. God Himself declared that David had served God's purpose for His own generation, and when his purpose was fulfilled, then and only then did he die.

Let's discover God's purpose for our lives, so that the declaration over our life, can be the same as that for King David.

Important Choices on the Journey to Purpose

Our purpose is <u>not</u> a point or a fixed position where we will one day arrive. Instead, our purpose is in our daily journey with God, and as we live each day, journeying with Him, He will move us to accomplish certain things that are all part of His plan and purpose for us.

We will not fulfill our purpose by solely focusing on a specific goal, and working hard to fulfill that goal. We will <u>only</u> find and fulfill our purpose as we journey with the Lord, and while on the journey He will continually lead us and present opportunities to us for us to accomplish, and for us to enjoy.

1. Choose To Enjoy Each Step in Your Journey

Romans 14:17, NIV - *For the <u>kingdom of God</u> is not a matter of eating and drinking, but of righteousness, peace and <u>joy</u> in the Holy Spirit.*

Even when we don't understand all that God is doing, we need to choose to trust Him, and enjoy the journey. This is the key to freeing our heart and mind of unnecessary burdens and worries.

2. Choose To Know the Father on Your Journey

John 17:3, NIV - *Now <u>this is eternal life</u>: <u>that they may know you, the only true God</u>, and Jesus Christ, whom you have sent.*

God's purpose for our life is directly tied to our relationship with Him in this life. Our purpose <u>FOR</u> the Lord cannot be separated from our purpose <u>IN</u> the Lord. <u>HE</u> is our purpose, and He is our companion <u>ON</u> our journey to purpose.

3. **Choose To Obey the Father on Your Journey**

Genesis 12:1, NIV - *The LORD had said to Abram, "Leave your country, your people and your father's household and <u>go to the land I will **show** you</u>."*

Day by day, as we live out our love for God by actively believing and obeying, our path and direction will become clearer. And at each step, we will be asked again to obey Him, and step out in faith for the next step.

4. **Choose to Focus on Your Journey, Not Someone Else's Journey**

Hebrews 12:1, NIV - *"... let us throw off everything that hinders and the sin that so easily entangles, and let us run with perseverance <u>the race marked out for **us**</u>."*

We should focus on our journey with God, for in it is our purpose. We should not try to copy or judge another person's journey. We need to simply focus on our journey.

5. **Choose To Live For God's Approval, Not Someone Else's Approval**

1 Thessalonians 2:4, NIV - *"On the contrary, we speak as <u>men approved by God</u> to be entrusted with the gospel. We are not trying to please men but God, who tests our hearts."*

2 Timothy 2:15, NIV - *"Do your best to <u>present yourself to God as one</u> [literally: who has already been] <u>approved</u>, a workman who does not need to be ashamed ..."*

We are to speak, to minister, and to live as those who have been approved by God. If we want to be in God's perfect will for our life, we cannot be someone who lives for the approval of others.

6. Choose to Accept Opposition as A Confirmation of The Father's Will

1 Corinthians 16:8-9, NIV - *"(8) But I will stay on at Ephesus until Pentecost, (9) because a great door for effective work has opened to me, and there are many who <u>oppose</u> me."*

Fulfilling our purpose and reaching a new level with God often means facing new opposition from the enemy. Opposition should never been seen as a sign from God to quit. It should be seen as a sign to pray, and seek clarity concerning God's will.

7. Choose To Persevere Through the Opposition

James 1:2-4, NIV - *(2) Consider it pure joy, my brothers, whenever you face <u>trials</u> of many kinds, (3) because you know that the testing of your faith develops <u>perseverance</u>. (4) <u>Perseverance must finish its work</u> so that <u>you may be mature and complete, not lacking anything</u>.*

Trials will come, and when they come, we will either break-through, or break-down. Perseverance is the God-given resource to help us break-through. Maturity and full resources only comes through perseverance.

8. Choose To Remember From Where Your Source of Victory Comes

1 Corinthians 15:57, NIV - *"But thanks be to <u>God</u>! He gives us the victory through our Lord Jesus Christ."*

1 John 4:4, NIV - *"<u>You</u>, dear children, are from God and <u>have overcome</u> them, because <u>the one who is in you is greater than the one who is in the world</u>."*

When seasons of difficulty come from the enemy, seasons of strength and promotion come from the Lord!

The devil isn't going to roll out the red carpet just because we decided to do something great for God. However, as we choose to allow God to be our source, the red carpet of the blood of Christ becomes our path to victory through every challenge.

9. **Choose To Keep the Eight Commitments**

- I commit to enjoy each step in my journey.
- I commit to know the Father on my journey.
- I commit to obey the Father on my journey.
- I commit to focus on my journey, not on someone else's journey.
- I commit to live for God's approval, not someone else's approval.
- I commit to accept opposition as a confirmation of the Fathers will.
- I commit to persevere through the opposition.
- I commit to remember from where my source of victory comes.

My P.U.R.P.O.S.E. — Seven Indicators

To discover your purpose – your God-given and God-ordained reason for His creating you and putting you on this earth – God has given us seven indicators. Taken together, these seven indicators point to a unified and focused purpose for your life.

 Your **Primary Passions** are those very specific things which God put within you that drive you, that inspire you, that energize you when you do them. God put these passions within you in order for you to love what you are called to do, and be energized when you do it.

 Your **Underlying Values** are those specific things that God placed in your heart that you truly care about, or value. They are the "bulls-eye" at which you are to aim with your life. They are the things in your heart for which you are truly willing to live your whole life.

 Your **Reoccurring Experiences** are those things that God moves you (knowingly or unknowingly) to experience over and over throughout your life. Because, "God works in you to will and to do His good pleasure...". They are part of your life's ministry for Him.

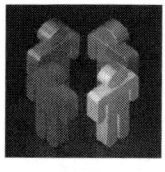 Your **Personality Traits** are your unique mix of relational characteristics that determine how you express yourself, and how you re-energize yourself. Knowing your personality will help you discover how you can best express your purpose with others.

 Your **Overriding Motivations** are those unique mix of "burdens of the heart" that motivate you to persevere when challenges come. They determine what realm of serving in which you will function most effectively, and be most comfortable, as you live out your purpose.

 Your **Spiritual Gifts** are your God-given empowerments that help you to express your purpose. They are like your special tools in your tool-kit that you have available to you, to fulfill your purpose more effectively and skilfully. Your Spiritual Gifts give practical expression to your purpose.

 Your **Extra Resources** are those extra talents and abilities that you have, that are either "wired" in you (ie. natural attributes) or learned skills (ie. skills which you were taught). These can be used to serve the needs of others, on the pathway to purpose.

Initial Diagnostic Questions

Primary Passions

God has placed certain passions within you, that when you do them, they keep you energized. These are indicators of the main expression of your primary purpose.

Questions:

- What activities energize you when you do them, or even think of doing them?
- What activities give you great enjoyment when you do them?
- What activities pull out the greatest creativity in you?
- What activities cause you the greatest satisfaction when you do them?
- What activities do you desire to do, even if you aren't paid to do them?

Underlying Values

God has placed specific things in the core of your heart that you value above everything else. These are the clearest indicators of your primary purpose.

Questions:

- What thing or things do you care for, beyond all others?
- What thing or things stir up righteous anger within you when they are left undone?
- What thing "calls to your heart" as something in which it is worth investing your life?
- What need in the world around you is a need for which you would give the rest of your life?

Reoccurring Experiences

God has led you through life into reoccurring opportunities and situations that indicate the primary environment or place that you are called to serve Him.

Questions:

- Do you keep finding yourself being put into the same place of serving others (eg. Leadership, administration, planning, decorating, counselling, encouraging, etc.)?
- Do you keep finding yourself working with the same type of people, or with the same needs?
- Do you keep having people come to you to request a certain type of assistance from you?
- Are you finding yourself becoming increasingly competent in a certain expression of service?

Personality Traits

Your God-formed personality indicates what type of group or situation in which you can most effectively be involved.
Questions:

- Based on my personality, am I most comfortable with individuals, small groups, or large groups?
- Based on my personality, am I more comfortable out in public, or working behind the scenes?
- Based on my personality, am I more effective working with people, or things?
- Based on my personality, am I more comfortable taking charge, or serving someone else?
- Based on my personality, am I more successful working with people, or projects?

Overriding Motivation

God has given each Christian an overriding ministry motivation that corresponds with one of the five-fold ministry gifts. These indicate the main expression of your ministry calling.

Questions:

- Based on the five-fold ministry list in Ephesians 4:11-12, would I rather express my service similar to that of an apostle, prophet, evangelist, pastor, or teacher?
- Which one of these five ministries, inspires and excites me the most?
- Which type of ministry am I most drawn to in other people (ie. Am I drawn to apostles, prophets, evangelists, pastors, or teachers).
- Which type of ministry expression have others most often invited me to serve?

Spiritual Gifts

God has given each person a "mix" of gifts (see Romans 12:6-8) that He wants you to use as tools for ministering to others. For example, if you have the gift of teaching, teaching is a tool that God has given you, to carry out your ministry calling.

Questions:

- Which of the following gifts am I most competent in using (prophetic preaching, serving, teaching, encouraging, sharing resources, leading, showing mercy)?
- Which is my top, second, and third gift?
- Which gifts do other people say I have?
- In which gifts do I most often have people request that I function?
- Which gifts most excite me?

- Which gifts do I find most easy to do, almost "second nature" to me?

Extra Resources (Talents, Skills, Abilities)

You have **natural talents** — things at which you are relatively good. You have **learned skills** — they didn't come naturally, but you have found yourself to be good at doing them. You have **physical abilities** — things that you can do, but may not be really effective, that God wants you to use to serve others, all in order to develop godly character in you as a servant of others.

Questions:

- What natural talents do I seem to possess that I can use for serving others (painting, drawing, singing, adding numbers, organizing, dancing, writing, etc.)?
- What learned skills have I developed that I can use for serving others (playing an instrument, building a home, cement work, electrical work, computer programming, photography, driving a truck, translating languages, etc.)?
- What physical abilities do I have that I can use for serving others (moving heavy objects, cleaning homes, delivering parcels, filing, answering the phone, etc.)?

First Impressions About My Purpose

My **P**rimary Passions (use verbs):

My **U**nderlying Values (use nouns):

My **R**eoccurring Experiences:

My **P**ersonality/Temperament:

My **O**verriding Motivation (choose top 2 from Ephesians 4:11-12):

My **S**piritual Gifts (choose top 3 from Romans 12:6-8):

My **E**xtra Resources (what can I do to begin to serve NOW?)

Section 2 – Passions And Values

Your Goal:

To discover your Primary Passions
and your Underlying Values
so that you can begin to
refocus your life.

<u>P</u>.U.R.P.O.S.E. — Discovering Your Primary Passions

Your Primary Passions are those very specific things which God put within you that drive you, that inspire you, that energize you when you do them. God put these passions within you in order for you to love what you are called to do, and be energized when you do it.

Defining Your Primary Passions

1. God Uses Our Primary Passions To Move Us Toward Our Purpose

a) Two Kinds Of Passions

Romans 8:5-8, NIV - *(5) For those who live according to the flesh set their minds on the things of the flesh, but those who live according to the Spirit, the things of the Spirit. (6) For to be carnally minded is death, but to be spiritually minded is life and peace. (7) Because the carnal mind is enmity against God; for it is not subject to the law of God, nor indeed can be. (8) So then, those who are in the flesh cannot please God.*

Galatians 5:24, NKJV - *And those who are Christ's have crucified the flesh with its passions and desires.*

Romans 7:5, NKJV - *For when we were in the flesh, the sinful passions which were aroused by the law were at work in our members to bear fruit to death.*

We have healthy passions, and unhealthy passions. We have passions motivated from the Holy Spirit, and passions motivated by our flesh. Passions of the flesh bear the fruit of sin and death. Passions of the Spirit bear the fruit of life and peace. God created our primary (healthy) passions.

b) God Created Our Primary Passions

Psalm 139:13, NIV - *For You created my inmost being; you knit me together in my mother's womb.*

Proverbs 23:16, NIV - *My inmost being will rejoice when your lips speak what is right.*

Our inmost being is that core place in our lives that gets excited or stirred up, when our passions are touched.

c) God Works With Our Passions

Titus 2:11-12, NIV - *(11) For the <u>grace of God</u> that brings salvation has appeared to all men. (12) It teaches us to <u>say "No" to ungodliness and worldly passions</u>, and to live self-controlled, upright and godly lives in this present age.*
The more we say yes to our godly passions, the more we come into line with God's plans and purpose for our lives.

d) God Stirs Up Our God-Given Passions, So That We Will Fulfill Our Purpose

Philippians 2:13, NIV – (13) *"... it is <u>God</u> who <u>works in you to will</u> and <u>to act</u> according to his good purpose."*

God created us for a purpose, then He put our passions within us so that we would enjoy our purpose, and then He works in us, and stirs up our desires or passions, so that we would be motivated to fulfill our purpose.

2. Our Passions Are Our Emotional Heartbeat

The Bible uses the term "heart" to refer to the center of our motivation, desires, hopes, interests, ambitions, dreams, affections, and inclinations. Our heart represents the source of all of our motivations - what we love to do, and what we care about most. Our heart determines three key things:

a) Our heart determines why we <u>say</u> the things we do.

Matthew 12:34, NIV – (34) *"... For <u>out of</u> the overflow of <u>the heart</u> the <u>mouth speaks</u>."*

b) Our heart determines why we <u>feel</u> the way we do.

Philippians 1:7, NIV – (7) *"It is right for me to <u>feel this way</u> about all of you, since I have you <u>in my heart</u> ..."*

c) Our heart determines why we <u>act</u> the way we do.

Proverbs 4:23, NIV – (23) *"Above all else, guard your <u>heart</u>, for it is the <u>wellspring of life</u>."*

What is in your heart, will determine what you do, and how far you go in life.

3. Our Service For God Should Flow Out Of Our Passions

a) We Are To Serve God With Our Passions

Romans 1:9, NIV – (9) *"God, whom I <u>serve</u> with my whole <u>heart</u> ..."*

1 Samuel 12:20, NIV – (20) *"... <u>serve</u> the LORD with all your <u>heart</u>."*

b) We Are To Do God's Will With Our Passions

Ephesians 6:6, NIV – (6) *"... doing the <u>will</u> of God from your <u>heart</u>."*

4. How Do We Know When We Are Serving God From Our Heart?

a) Enthusiasm

2 Corinthians 8:17, NIV - *For Titus not only welcomed our appeal, but he is coming to you with much <u>enthusiasm</u> and on his own initiative.*

When we are doing what we love, no one has to motivate or challenge or check up on us, we do it out of sheer enjoyment.

b) Effectiveness

1 Corinthians 16:9, NIV – *A great door for <u>effective</u> work has opened to me, and there are many who oppose me.*

Whenever we do what God wired us to do, what we are passionate about, we get good at it. Passion drives perfection!

c) Fulfillment / Satisfaction

Ecclesiastes 3:13, NIV – *That everyone may eat and drink, and <u>find satisfaction</u> in all his toil -- <u>this is the gift of God</u>.*

There is a satisfaction or fulfillment that comes when we are serving according to our passion.

5. Summary

Your passions reveal the real you -- what you truly are, not what others think you are, or what circumstances force you to be.

Your passions are what you love to do -- what God gave you a heart to do.

Diagnostic Tool To Help You Define Your Primary Passions

God has placed certain passions within you, that when you do them, they keep you energized.

These are indicators of the main expression of your ministry calling.

1. Initial Questions About Your Primary Passions

- What activities energize you when you do them, or even think of doing them?
- What activities give you great enjoyment when you do them?
- What activities pull out the greatest creativity from you?
- What activities cause you the greatest satisfaction when you do them?
- What activities do you desire to do, even if you aren't paid to do them?

2. Our Passions Drive Us to Action

To fulfill our purpose, we need passion to act, and passion to persevere. Our God-given passions move us to act, and energize us as we act.

3. Primary Passions (Verbs)

Every purpose requires action, and action words are verbs. Which are the verbs that are most meaningful and purposeful for you, and which really excite and energize you?

Circle all of the verbs which really "connect" with you. If you want a verb that isn't in this list, feel free to add it. (Note: Remember to read each of these words as a verb, not as a noun.)

Activate   Advance   Affirm   Alleviate   Amaze   Anchor
Appreciate   Arrange   Believe   Bless   Brighten   Build
Call   Cause   Challenge   Champion   Circulate   Claim
Collect   Combine   Compel   Complete   Compose
Communicate   Conceive   Confirm   Contact   Counsel
Create   Defend   Delight   Deliver   Demonstrate
Develop   Devise   Direct   Discover   Distribute   Drive
Educate   Embody   Embrace   Empower   Encourage
Engage   Engineer   Enhance   Enlighten   Enlist
Enliven   Entertain   Envision   Equip   Evaluate   Excite
Explore   Express   Extend   Facilitate   Finance   Foster
Further   Gather   Give   Grant   Heal   Help   Hold
Host   Identify   Ignite   Illuminate   Immerse   Impart
Implement   Improve   Improvise   Increase   Inspire
Integrate   Involve   Keep   Know   Labour   Launch
Lead   Master   Mature   Measure   Model   Mould
Motivate   Move   Nurture   Open   Organize   Perform
Persuade   Possess   Prepare   Present   Produce
Progress   Promote   Provide   Radiate   Reach   Realize
Reclaim   Reduce   Refine   Reflect   Reform   Relate
Release   Renew   Resonate   Restore   Return   Reveal
Revise   Revive   Safeguard   Satisfy   Save   Serve
Shake-Up   Share   Speak   Stand   Strengthen
Summon   Support   Sustain   Take   Tap   Teach
Team   Touch   Train   Transform   Translate
Understand   Uphold   Unite   Utilize   Validate   Value
Venture   Verbalize   Work   Worship   Write   Yield

_____   _____

_____   _____

4. Twelve Verbs Which Connect With Me

Transfer the top **twelve** verbs (maximum) circled under point 3, "Primary Passions (Verbs)" to the spaces below.

_____   _____

_____   _____

_____   _____

_____   _____

_____   _____

_____   _____

5. Seven Verbs Which Inspire Me

From your new list of "Twelve Verbs Which Connect With Me", select the **seven** verbs from this list which most excite and inspire you, and write them below.

_____   _____

_____   _____

_____   _____

_____

6. **Three Verbs Most Like Me**

   From your new list of "Seven Verbs Which Excite And Inspire Me", select the **three** verbs that you feel are most like you when you read them (your three most meaningful, purposeful and exciting verbs), and write them below.

   _____   _____

   _____

7. **Write a sentence or two about what each of the three key verbs mean to you.**

   1. _____ :

   2. _____ :

   3. _____ :

   Please Note: Make note of these Primary Passions (Verbs). You will be using them later in this workbook.

8. Left Brain verses Right Brain

This method works very well for "left-brain" people – people who are more logical, concrete thinkers. However, if you are "right-brain" – a person who is more abstract and creative, try the following methods:

- Close your eyes and image yourself doing something really exciting, something that you really enjoy, and that excites you when you do it. What are you doing? Write down the "verbs" that best describe what you are doing.

- Draw a picture that excites you, a picture of yourself doing something that you are passionate about. What are you doing in the picture, and what about your activity excites you? Write down the "verbs" that best describe what you are doing.

P.U.R.P.O.S.E. — Discovering Your Underlying Values

Your Underlying Values are those specific things that God placed in your heart about which you truly care. They are the "bulls-eye" that you are to aim at with your life. They are the things in your heart for which you are truly willing to live and die.

Understanding The Kingdom Concept Of "Value"

1. The Kingdom Is Like Searching For and Receiving Something of Great Value

Matthew 13:45-46, NIV - *"(45) Again, the <u>kingdom</u> of heaven is <u>like</u> a <u>merchant looking for fine pearls</u>. (46) When he found one of <u>great value</u>, he went away and <u>sold everything</u> he had and bought it.*

a) The Merchant Was Focused On A Specific Treasure

   The merchant was looking for pearls, but not just any pearl. He was looking for "fine pearls". And he was even more discriminating. He focused on the one of "great value". How do we determine what is of great value?

b) The Merchant Was Discerning Of True Value

   In order for the merchant to choose the best pearl, he had to be able to discern between flawed pearls, common pearls, and pearls of great value. Discernment is necessary if we are to attain the truly valuable things in life.

c) The Merchant Was Committed To Pay the Price

   Even before the merchant started looking, he had already committed in his heart to pay the price when he found the pearl of great value. We often settle for less, because we are unwilling to pay the price to pursue the best. God wants us to start to value the things He values, and to discover the values He has put within us.

d) The Merchant Was Patient

Finding the fine things, the best things, the things of greatest value, takes time. The common things are always in greater supply than the things of great value. Are we patient enough to wait for the best?

2. The Kingdom Is Like A Treasure Hidden In A Field

Matthew 13:44, NIV - *"The kingdom of heaven is like treasure hidden in a field. When a man found it, he hid it again, and then in his joy went and sold all he had and bought that field."*

a) The Man Knew Where To Look

If you are going to find a treasure, you must have some idea of where to look. He knew to look in a field, but not just any field. How much time do we waste looking in the wrong places?

b) The Man Could Recognize True Treasure.

The man was familiar enough with treasure, that he could spot fake treasure, counterfeit treasure, and worthless treasure, from true treasure. How do we evaluate true treasure?

c) The Man Knew That The Specific Field Increased The Value Of The Treasure.

The man didn't just want the treasure. He also wanted the field. The treasure made the field more valuable, and the field made the treasure more valuable. Often it is the environment or the specific context that makes the treasure of great value. Are we concerned with the "where" as well as the "what"?

3. There Is A Treasure In Us To Be Discovered

    a) We Are God's Field

        1 Corinthians 3:9, NIV - *"For we are God's fellow workers; you are <u>God's field</u> ..."*

        We are God's field. God wants our whole field, not just the treasure in us.

    b) There Is A Treasure In Our Field

        2 Corinthians 4:7, NIV - *"But we have <u>this treasure in jars of clay</u> to show that this all-surpassing power is from God and not from us."*

        God has put a treasure inside each one of us. He wants us to discover it, discern its true value, and use it for His glory.

4. How Do We Recognize The Treasure? ... It Has Our Heart (Passion)

Matthew 6:21, NIV - *"For where your <u>treasure</u> is, there your <u>heart</u> will be also."*

The things that God truly wants us to "treasure" or value, tend to grip our heart. What inside us grips our heart as precious and of high value?

5. Underlying Values Defined

An underlying value is a driving desire or priority that God has placed inside us to help us to know where to aim our life. If we choose to follow God, they will become the driving force of our life. If we identify and pursue our God-given values, we'll unleash our potential and set ourselves up for fulfillment and success, because only when what's inside (our underlying values) lines up with what's outside, can we hope to accomplish what God has called us to do.

Examples Of Things We Should All Value

1. Faith

Hebrews 4:2, NIV - *"For we also have had the gospel preached to us, just as they did; but the message they heard was of no value to them, because those who heard did not combine it with faith."*

2. Love

Galatians 5:6, NIV - *"For in Christ Jesus neither circumcision nor uncircumcision has any value. The only thing that counts [has value] is faith expressing itself through love."*

3. Godliness

1 Timothy 4:8, NIV - *"For physical training is of some value, but godliness has value for all things, holding promise for both the present life and the life to come."*

4. Righteousness, Endurance, Gentleness, Peace

1 Timothy 6:11, NIV – *(11) But you, man of God, flee from all this, and pursue righteousness, godliness, faith, love, endurance and gentleness.*

2 Timothy 2:22, NIV – *(22) Flee the evil desires of youth, and pursue righteousness, faith, love and peace, along with those who call on the Lord out of a pure heart.*

If we are told to pursue these things, obviously they must have value.

Examples Of Underlying Values

1. Abraham - Reward From God

Hebrews 11:26, NIV – *"He regarded disgrace for the sake of Christ as of greater value than the treasures of Egypt, because he was <u>looking ahead to his reward</u>."*

Abraham was willing to face personal disgrace because he valued reward from God as more precious than the physical treasures of Egypt.

2. King David – Intimacy With God

Psalm 27:4, NIV - *One thing I ask of the LORD, this is what I seek: that I may dwell in the house of the LORD all the days of my life, to <u>gaze upon the beauty of the LORD</u> and to <u>seek him in his temple</u>.*

David's "one thing" of greatest value was intimacy with God, where He could experience God's beautiful character.

3. King Solomon - Wisdom and Understanding

Proverbs 4:5-7, NIV - *<u>Get wisdom, get understanding</u>: do not forget my words or swerve from them. Do not forsake wisdom, and she will protect you; love her, and she will watch over you. <u>Wisdom is supreme</u>; <u>therefore get wisdom</u>. Though it cost all you have, <u>get understanding</u>.*

King Solomon, after amassing great wealth, came to the conclusion that wisdom and understanding were of even greater value.[16]

4. Mother Teresa - Compassion For The Poor

"Loneliness and the feeling of being unwanted is the most terrible poverty."[17]

"'We think sometimes that poverty is only being hungry, naked, and homeless. The poverty of being unwanted, unloved, and uncared for is the greatest poverty. We must start in our own homes to remedy this kind of poverty."[18]

"If you can't feed a hundred people, then feed just one."[19]

"I try to give to the poor people for love what the rich could get for money. No, I wouldn't touch a leper for a thousand pounds; yet I willingly cure him for the love of God."[20]

"Our life of poverty is as necessary as the work itself. Only in heaven will we see how much we owe to the poor for helping us to love God better because of them."

5. Billy Graham - Spreading The Gospel

"Make sure of your commitment to Jesus Christ, and seek to follow Him every day. Don't be swayed by the false values and goals of this world, but put Christ and His will first in everything you do."[21]

"God proved His love on the Cross. When Christ hung, and bled, and died, it was God saying to the world, 'I love you.'"[22]

6. John Arnott - Experiencing The Father's Love And Giving It Away

"There is the need for an intimate romantic relationship with the Father. Abundant joy and an intimate personal receiving of God's love should be our priority because you can never get enough of this, people return again and again to swim in the river or soak in the son (Jesus)."[23]

"Wouldn't it be great if there were somewhere you could go and just get really filled up with power and love, the love of God? But it doesn't stop there. What happens is, there's a transference of His anointing where, not only do you see it, not only do you experience it for yourself, but you're going to take it home to your people."[24]

How To Uncover Your Underlying Values

1. **Separate Your "Practiced" Values From Your "Claimed" Values**

   a) Identity the Biblical values that apply to everyone - God's moral values which are non-optional.

   Biblical values apply to everyone. They are non-negotiable, and so do not indicate your underlying values.

   b) Identify and write down the specific values that define you.

   Identify those things that are always true of you, no matter what the situation, no matter who is in the room.

   c) Compare your written values (convictions) with your practiced values

   If you do not live out your written values, then they are not your true values. They may be "convictions", but not your true values. Your true underlying values will drive your actions and behaviour.

2. **Use The Negative - What Things Really Anger You?**

   You can discover your underlying values by looking at the negative, those negative things in life that really anger you. For example:

   - Hypocrisy (therefore you value integrity)
   - Selfishness (therefore you value generosity)
   - Pretension (therefore you value authenticity)
   - Half-heartedness (therefore you value excellence)
   - Rudeness (therefore you value kindness)

3. **Use The Positive - What Things Bring You Much Enjoyment?**

You can discover your underlying values by looking at the positive, those positive things in life that give you great joy and satisfaction. For example:

- Spending time with outcasts (mercy)
- Teaching (education)
- Playing with children (children)
- Helping people (service)
- Arranging flowers (beauty)

Diagnostic Tool To Help You Define Your Underlying Values

1. Underlying Values (Nouns)

Your God-given underlying values give you focus. Underlying Values are objects on which to focus, and so <u>Underlying Values are nouns</u>. Which of these nouns do you most want to represent in this world? For which of these concepts or principles would you be willing to live your whole life, to sacrifice for?

Circle all of the nouns which really "connect" with you. If you think of a noun that is not in this list, feel free to add it. (Note: Remember to read each of these words as a noun, not as a verb).

Accountability   Adventure   Attitude   Authenticity
Beacon   Boldness   Change   Character   Charity
Collaboration   Compassion   Confidence   Courage
Creativity   Dedication   Devotion   Dignity   Discipleship
Discipline   Discovery   Diversity   Efficiency   Empathy
Encouragement   Endurance   Enthusiasm   Equality
Evangelism   Excellence   Excitement   Faith
Faithfulness   Family   Fellowship   Freedom   Generosity
Gentleness   Godliness   Goodness   Government   Grace
Gratefulness   Growth   Healing   Honesty   Honour
Hope   Humility   Humour   Inner Peace   Integrity
Intimacy   Joy   Justice   Kindness   Knowing   God
Leadership   Learning   Legacy   Love   Loyalty   Maturity
Mercy   Nobility   Obedience   Openness   Order
Passion   Patience   Peace   Perseverance   Personal
Growth   Positive Attitude   Prayer   Privilege   Purity
Purpose   Recovery   Relationships   Reliability   Respect
Sacrifice   Safety   Security   Self-control   Self-discipline
Self-esteem   Selflessness   Self-respect   Self-worth
Servanthood   Servant-leadership   Service   Simplicity

Steadfastness   Stewardship   Submission
Teachableness   Teamwork   Thankfulness   Transparency
Trust   Trustworthiness   Truth   Unity   Value   Well-
being   Wisdom   Wholeness   Worship   Zeal

_____   _____

_____   _____

2. Ten Nouns Which Connect With Me

Transfer the top **ten** nouns (maximum) circled under point 1, "Underlying Values (Nouns)" to the spaces below.

_____   _____

_____   _____

_____   _____

_____   _____

_____   _____

3. Three Nouns Which Inspire Me

From your new list of "Ten Nouns Which Connect With Me", select the **three** nouns from this list which most excite and inspire you, and write them below.

_____   _____

_____

4. **One Noun Most Like Me**

   From your new list of "Three Nouns Which Inspire Me", select the one core value (noun) that you feel is most like you when you read it (your one most meaningful, purposeful and exciting one), and write it below.

   _____

5. **Write a sentence or two about what the key noun means to you.**

   _____:

Please Note: Make note of this Underlying Value (Noun). You will be using it later in this workbook.

Section 3 – Developing Your Mission Statement

Your Goal:

To develop a written-down reason for living,
so that you can begin to address the
Why, What, Where, and How of life.

Good News — God Wants Us To Enjoy Our Work!

1. We Are Called To Joyfully Work At Leaving An Inheritance

Ecclesiastes 3:22, NIV - *"So I saw that there is nothing better for a man than to enjoy his work, because that is his lot."*

- "Enjoy" = "samach" (Hebrew) = "rejoice in, be joyful in, be glad in"
- 'Work" = "maaseh" (Hebrews) = "deed, work, workmanship, accomplishments"
- "Lot" = "cheleq" (Hebrew) - "portion (of land), territory, inheritance"

Our portion, our inheritance, is to experience great joy as we accomplish deeds according to our purpose.

2. We Are To Enjoy And Reap Prosperity In The Work Of Our Calling

Ecclesiastes 5:18, NIV- *"Then I realized that it is good and proper for a man to eat and drink, and to find satisfaction in his toilsome labor under the sun during the few days of life God has given him -- for this is his lot."*

- "Proper" = "yapheh" (Hebrew) = "fair, appropriate, beautiful"
- "Find satisfaction" = "tobah" (Hebrew) = "welfare, benefit, good things, prosperity"
- "Toilsome labour" = "amal" (Hebrew) = "trouble, labor, toil, hard work, mischief (playful fun)"
- "Lot" = "cheleq" (Hebrew) - "portion (of land), territory, inheritance"

It is very appropriate that we experience enjoyment and prosperity if we work hard in our area of purpose.

3. **God Imparts Abilities Into Us So That We Are Empowered To Fulfill, With Joy, The Work We Are Called To Do**

Ecclesiastes 5:19, NIV - *"Moreover, when God gives any man wealth and possessions, and enables him to enjoy them, to accept his lot and be happy in his work -- this is a gift of God."*

- "Gives" = "nathan" (Hebrew) = "gives, put in, sets in place, imparts, appoints, enables, entrusts"
- 'Wealth" = "nekes" (Hebrew) = "riches, treasures, abundant resources"
- "Enables" = "shalat" (Hebrew) = "give the ability to master or exercise authority over, to gain mastery over or have dominion over"
- "Enjoy" = "samach" (Hebrew) = "rejoice in, be joyful in, be glad in"
- "Accept" = "nasa" (Hebrew) = "lift up, carry, take, bear, bring forth"
- "Lot" = "cheleq" (Hebrew) = "portion (of land), territory, inheritance"
- `Work" = "amal" (Hebrew) = "trouble, labour, toil, hard work, mischief (playful fun)"
- "Gift" = "mattath" (Hebrew) = from "Nathan" (Hebrew) = "gives, put in, sets in place, imparts, appoints, enables, entrusts"

God imparts abundant resources and abilities into us so that we can joyfully accept and bring forth fruitfulness in our lives according to our purpose.

4. **Our Purpose Is To Be Fulfilled Within A Certain Field Or Sphere Of Ministry Influence**

2 Corinthians 10:13, NIV - *'We, however, will not boast beyond proper limits, but will confine our boasting to the field God has assigned to us, a field that reaches even to you."*

- "Proper limits" = "metron" (Greek) = a measure, a size of influence
- "Field" = "kano_n" (Greek) = a place of ruling, a sphere of influence
- "Assigned" = "merizo" (Greek) = to divide up, to assign, to give a portion

God assigns us to a certain purpose within a certain sphere of work where we can be effective and influence others according to God's will.

What Is A Mission Statement?

A mission statement is, in essence, a written-down reason for being - whether for a person or for a company. It is the key to finding your path in life.

Webster's College Dictionary gives several definitions of the word "mission." Among them are:

- a specific task that a person or group of persons is sent to perform;
- the place of work of such persons, or the territory of their responsibility;
- a military operational task, usually assigned by a higher headquarters;
- an aerospace operation designed to carry out the goals of a specific program;
- an allotted or self-imposed duty or task; a calling.

A mission statement is a written-down reason for your existence - whether for a person or for an organization. A mission statement becomes a clear tool to find your path in life, and identify the purpose that God created you to follow and fulfill. Having a clearly written mission statement gives you a guide that you can use to initiate, evaluate, and refine all of your activities.

While mission statements have only recently become popular, they have actually been around for centuries. Two thousand years ago, Jesus declared His mission statement in a single sentence.

John 10:10, NKJV – "... *I have come that they may have life, and that they may have it more abundantly."*

He then clarified that mission statement for those around Him.

John 12:46-47, NIV – *"I have come into the world as a light, so that no one who believes in me should stay in darkness. As for the* *person who hears my words but does not keep them, I do not judge him. For <u>I did not come to judge the world, but to save it</u>.* [i.e.. <u>to give life, and life more abundantly</u>]."

Everything that Jesus did, whether ministering to children, turning water into wine, teaching people at the seashore, or challenging the corrupt religious system ... Jesus did because of His mission statement. His mission statement not only covered His work (ministry) life, but also His personal and leisure time, as well. It also helped Him determine and focus His activities. When the woman caught in adultery was brought before Him, He refused to judge her, because His mission was not to condemn, but to give life. Knowing His mission helped Him decide how to act (and not act), what to do (and not do), and even what to say (and not say) when challenging situations arose.

All Great Leaders Had a Mission Statement

The truth is that all great leaders in history have had mission statements that were no more than a single sentence long.

- Abraham Lincoln - preserve the Union.
- Franklin D. Roosevelt - end the Depression.
- Nelson Mandela - end apartheid.
- Mother Teresa - show mercy and compassion to the dying.
- Joan of Arc - free France.
- Nehemiah - rebuild the walls of Jerusalem.
- Paul - bring the gospel to the Gentiles.

Why Have A Mission Statement?

Having a clearly defined mission statement gives a person a description of purpose that can be used to initiate, evaluate, and refine all of their activities.

1. They Help Us Have a Meaningful Life

Caty Medrano writes that the top human fear is fear of failure.[25] Richard Leider and David Shapiro say that the number one fear is living a meaningless life.[26] Genevieve Bell says that humanity's greatest fear is about being irrelevant.[27]

What do all of these findings have in common? People have a deep need to fulfill a meaningful and relevant purpose. So discovering our purpose and fulfilling it is probably the most important activity that we can pursue.

2. They Help Us To Become Effective In Life

Consider for a moment the cost of not having a clearly defined purpose or mission in life. Crime, unemployment, depression, suicide, inefficiency, lack of focus. The emotional, psychological, and spiritual consequences are enormous.

Now imagine what the world would be like if each and every person on the earth had a clearly defined purpose and mission statement and was committed to working full time to fulfill it. Work absenteeism would drop. Productivity would soar. All corporate and government rhetoric would become meaningful action. Unfulfillment would turn into satisfaction. Depression would turn into passion. Frustration would turn into energy. Every problem to avoid would become a challenge to overcome.

Research has shown that people with carefully and clearly defined missions have always led or surpassed those who don't have one.

3. **They Help Us To Make Good Choices**

In this world we are daily forced to make decisions that will either lead us closer to, or further from our goals, and our mission in life. Because of that reality, no tool can be as valuable in providing clear direction as a mission statement. Each one of us needs a brief, concise, and focused statement of purpose that we can use to initiate, evaluate, and refine all of our activities. A carefully thought-out personal mission statement acts as both a yoke and a knife — it yokes us to what is important in our life, and it cuts away all of the unimportant.

4. **They Help Us To Do What We Are Called To Do**

Because of the pressure of family, friends, and society on a person's life, you can be sure that you will either be living your mission, or you will be living someone else's. Having a mission statement can help you to choose which it will be.

5. **They Help Us To Choose The Best Career**

Knowing our personal mission statement helps us choose the best career path. Once we are clear about what we were put here to do, then our "jobs" become only a means toward our purpose, not an end in themselves.

6. **They Help Us To Develop Beneficial Relationships**

Having and knowing our personal mission statement can also help us to more purposefully make and nurture relationships that move us toward fulfilling our purpose.

7. **They Help Us To Persevere Through Challenging Situations**

Having a personal mission statement has been shown, in fact, to be the one thing that can keep someone alive in settings as brutal and life-threatening as concentration camps.

8. **They Help Give Us Peace Of Mind**

Here is one person's testimony: "In my own life I found that once I developed a mission statement that was broad enough to cover my interests and activities both on and off 'the job,' my life began to make a dramatic shift. Decision-making came more easily, because now I had something against which to measure my activities. I learned firsthand the terror and majesty and power of having an exciting mission statement — one that says 'This is what I am about.' I began to shed my fears about losing or not having a job, since I knew I would always have my mission, and any job I got would have to be an expression of that."

Connecting My Passions And Values Defines My Mission

Our **underlying value** is the target – the bullseye – that thing at which we are called to aim.

Our **primary passions** are the things that we love to do – the arrows – that we will use to reach or hit our target, and keep us motivated as we work toward it.

When our primary passions and our underlying values connect, we will fulfill our **purpose**, and our purpose is our mission in life.

Three Elements To A Good Mission Statement

There are three simple elements to a good mission statement.

1. **A mission statement should be short.**

   A mission statement should be no more than a single sentence long. We must be able to communicate our mission concisely, so that people (including us) can relate to it, and remember it.

2. **A mission statement should be clear.**

   A mission statement should be so clear, that it could be easily communicated and understood and repeated by a twelve-year-old.

3. **A mission statement should be memorable.**

   A mission statement should be so memorable, that it can be recited by memory, even under stress in the case of an extreme emergency.

   As Christians, we are each given a life-changing, world-shaking mission from God, a mission to impact others for the cause of Christ. Certainly, we, more than any others on the face of this earth, should be able to communicate what is our mission in life.

Ten Flawed Beliefs About Your "Mission"

1. "My job is my mission."

Your job may be and ideally should be part of your mission, but a mission is always more encompassing than just a job.

Acts 18:2-3, NIV — *(2) There he met a Jew named Aquila, a native of Pontus, who had recently come from Italy with his wife Priscilla, because Claudius had ordered all the Jews to leave Rome. Paul went to see them, (3) and because <u>he was a tentmaker</u> as they were, he stayed and worked with them.*

Paul was a tentmaker, as were Aquila and Priscilla. They used tent making to finance their ministry, and also to build relational bridges to each community where they went. However, their job was not their ministry, simply a tool to finance their ministry.

So realize that jobs change, maybe you don't like your job, maybe you only have a temporary job, maybe you just took your job to pay off some bills, or it was the only job available, but that doesn't mean you have to be stuck in that job forever.

2. "My role is my mission."

One's role, both personal and professional, may change over the course of life, and so you should never define your mission by a single role.

1 Timothy 2:7, NIV - *"And for this purpose I was appointed a herald and an apostle ... and a teacher of the true faith to the Gentiles."*

Paul had three different roles or functions depending on the circumstances. Sometimes his role was that of a herald. Sometimes it was that of an apostle. Sometimes it was that of a teacher. But his mission was to bring the gospel to the Gentiles.

Your role is the present position or function that you fulfill, and which may or may not change from year to year. Your mission is your goal in life, which will never change. Your present role may or may not line up with your mission. Your mission is much bigger than a temporary role.

3. **"My present responsibilities are my mission."**

Often people's present responsibilities fall under the realm of urgent, but not genuinely important.

Mark 12:33, NIV - *"To love him with all your heart, with all your understanding and with all your strength, and to love your neighbor as yourself is more important than all burnt offerings and sacrifices."*

Making sacrifices is important, and often needs to be done, but loving God and people is more important.

So often, what we are presently doing may need to be done, but isn't really part of what we should be spending our lives doing, in the long term. Your mission is much bigger than your present responsibilities.

4. **"I presently can not fulfill my mission."**

To fulfill your mission, you may not need massive changes in your life, but instead, just an increased awareness of the importance of your daily tasks and choices.

Ephesians 3:20, NIV - *"Now to him who is able to do immeasurably more than all we ask or imagine, according to his power that is at work within us."*

God's power is in you to accomplish great things, so that often, making a few different choices each day, which are more in line with your mission, will allow you to fulfill your mission in life.

5. **"I am not important enough to have a mission."**

Every word we speak, every action we take, has an effect on the totality of humanity.

Romans 14:7, NIV - *(7) For none of us lives to himself alone and none of us dies to himself alone.*

No one is invisible, and so everything we do is noticed by someone, and affects someone, either positively, or negatively. For example, Paul Revere's blacksmith was indispensable, and yet what he did largely went unnoticed.

Every person is important to God. And every person has a mission to fulfil.

6. **"I need a big mission in order for it to be important"**

No mission is too small, and no mission is too big. If we raise or teach or heal one creature, our life can be considered a success. Who led Billy Graham to the Lord? You may not know his name, but that does not make him unimportant. Because of him, millions have come to Christ through his convert (and perhaps his only convert) Billy Graham.

Zechariah 4:10, NIV - *(10) Who despises the day of small things? . . .*

Small things to us, are big things to God. And if fulfilled, they may lead to many more.

7. **"A mission must require much sacrifice and suffering to be from God."**

Matthew 11:29-30, NASB - *"Take my yoke upon you, and learn of me; for I am meek and lowly in heart; and you shall find rest unto your souls. For my <u>yoke is easy</u>, and my <u>burden is light</u>."*

Your mission doesn't need to cause you to suffer. Jesus said that when you took the right yoke on your life, it would be easier, and lighter, not more difficult, and heavier. You don't have to always suffer, to serve God.

8. **"My mission must be the same as my peers in order to be valid."**

You must temporarily distance yourself from the influence of those around you, when developing your personal mission statement.

Romans 12:2, GNB - *"Do not conform yourselves to the standards of this world, but let God transform you ..."*

We try so hard not to be influenced by the standards of this world, and its pressure on us to be like it wants us to be. Yet we often conform ourselves to the expectations of our friends. And often what our friends expect from us, even our godly friends, may keep us from our life's mission.

You are unique, and so your mission will be unique.

9. **"My location determines my mission."**

In most cases, you can fulfill your mission anywhere ... in any place, and in any environment. What is important, is that what you are doing on a daily basis, is in line with your mission.

Acts 13:36, NIV — *"For when David had served God's purpose in his own generation, he fell asleep."*

When David was on the hills at night looking after sheep, he was fulfilling his mission. When he was playing a harp for Saul, he was fulfilling his mission. When he was running for his life from Saul, he was fulfilling his mission. And when he was sitting on a throne as King, he was fulfilling his mission.

You don't have to move to serve God and fulfill your calling. But you must be in the right environment to fulfill your destiny. Your mission is to your generation (a people), not to your geography (location).

10. "I can't get any closer to my mission."

Look carefully to see if you are taking a job that runs parallel to your true heart's desire and mission – but is not actually the "real thing".

Matthew 4:19, NIV - *"Come, follow me," Jesus said, "and I will make you fishers of men."*

There's a big difference between fishing for fish, and winning people to the Lord Jesus Christ. Or is there? Both require long hours, hard work, patience, and perseverance. Both require being able to read the "water" to know the best place and time to catch "fish". Both require being able to skillfully bring in the "catch" without losing it.

There are often two streams in life; the one in which you are, and the one that runs next to it, in which you should be. Sometimes just small adjustments will move you to where you need to be. For example, you may need to change from writing advertisements to writing books. You may need to change from being a mechanic to being a test driver. Or perhaps you need to change from selling art supplies, to painting pictures.

You were born with the potential to fulfill a great destiny. It is up to you to embrace it. God has a destiny for each one of us.

Jeremiah 29:11, NIV — *(11) For I know the plans I have for you, "declares the LORD," plans to prosper you and not to harm you, plans to give you hope and a future.*

Mission Statement Work Sheet

Remember, this is a work in progress, and the words may not yet fit together or sound exactly right, until you adjust them a bit.

1. Transfer Your Verbs

Transfer your "Seven Verbs Which Inspire Me" and your "Three Verbs Most Like Me" that you selected in the Primary Passions section.

a) Seven Verbs Which Inspire Me

_____   _____

_____   _____

_____   _____

_____

b) Three Verbs Most Like Me

_____   _____

_____

2. Transfer Your Nouns

Transfer your "Three Nouns Which Inspire Me" and your "One Noun Most Like Me" that you selected in the Underlying Value section.

a) Three Nouns Which Inspire Me

_____   _____

_____

b) One Noun Most Like Me

_____

3. Combine Your Primary Passions and Underlying Value

Transfer your working combination of your Primary Passions (your 3 action verbs) and your Underlying Value (your 1 noun) to the blanks below.

My mission is to:

_____, _____, and _____
(your three Action Verbs — your Primary Passions)

_____
(your one Noun — your Underlying Value)

4. Adjust Your Primary Passions And Underlying Value.

a) Combine each primary passion with your underlying value.

Combine each primary passion (verb) one at a time, with the underlying value (noun) -- asking the questions below.

- What about that word (verb) do I like?
- Is that what I really do or want to do?
- What other words might make a better substitute?

b) Replace a primary passion if necessary.

If one or more of the verbs is weak or doesn't make sense with the core value, ask yourself which word(s) rings more true for you, and then discard or lay aside the weaker word and seek a stronger replacement. Remember that you have other primary passions (verbs) which you can still draw from.

c) Example[28]:

One man said his core value was "people." He had been unable to come up with any verbs. The question was asked – "What about people (core value) do you like?" "Everything," he said. What especially excites you about people (core value)? "Seeing them come together," he replied. "In a team?" I asked. "Yes," he said excitedly. "What would those teams be about?" I asked. "Healing," he replied. It boiled down that his mission is "to create, lead, and inspire healing teams." "That's what he does!" shouted one of his co-workers. The man brightened visibly and I asked, "If you could do this - and only this – would you be happy?" "Yes," he replied. "Would you be busy?" "Yes," he said. "Could you do this at work and at home?" "Yes," he stated. We had discovered his mission statement!

Strengthening Your Mission Statement

A good mission statement will be inspiring, exciting, clear, true, and appealing.

1. **Check The Combination (Logic And Flow) Of The Words**

    You may want to have a partner help you with this exercise.

    Can you _____ _____
    (primary passion #1 - verb) (underlying value - noun)?

    Can you _____ _____
    (primary passion #2 - verb) (underlying value - noun)?

    Can you _____ _____
    (primary passion #3 - verb) (underlying value - noun)?

2. **Check The Legitimacy Of The Words - Is It You? (Yes/No)**

    a) Y/N   Does this mission describe you? (Does it describe how you are?)

    b) Y/N   Is this mission true of you? (Does it describe what is important to you?)

    c) Y/N   Would you be willing to have your life be about this and only this?

    d) Y/N   Can you confidently declare this as an accurate statement about yourself?

    e) Y/N   Does this mission excite you? (Does it inspire you?)

    f) Y/N   Does it excite others? (Ask others who know you)

    g) Y/N   Can you do this at your place of employment?

h) Y/N   Can you do this in your home?

i) Y/N   Can you do this at a social gathering (At a party?)

j) Y/N   Can you do this by yourself (When you are alone)?

3. **Check The Inspiration Level Of The Words**

   Unsuccessful or inadequate mission statements are:

   a) Uninspiring.

      For example: "To survive"; "To exist"; "To get by"; To retire by the age of fifty-five"

   b) Limited to the benefit of only one person or one group of people (including yourself).

      For example: "To conquer Europe"; "To beat Toronto"; "To own a Mercedes"; "To put the competition out of business"

   c) Unintelligible to other people.

      For example, they may be too long, or not clear, or not to the point.

   d) Full of clichés, slogans, or ordinary phrases which are spoken without any passion.

      For example: 'We are here to serve our customers", "To provide high quality service", "To be an organization of excellence", "To give the best service", "To be a top-ten sales person", "to get to the top".

4. **What If Your New Mission Statement Just Doesn't Seem To Describe You?**

    If you get too baffled, stop and ask 'What is it I want to be about?" At this point you can usually say in a sentence or two what your heart is feeling. Listen carefully to yourself — selecting out the adjectives and phrases and listening only for verbs and nouns.

    Listen carefully to yourself — and pay attention to the verbs and nouns you used.

5. **Print Out You Mission Statement And Post It In A Visible Spot**

Determining Your Target Group

Discover who you are called to serve, be with, inspire, influence, learn from, and be affected by.

Some people will have a clearly defined target group, but others may not. For example, your target group may be people in general, or it may be a specific group, like children, the elderly, the divorced, the handicapped, the abused, the discouraged, the hopeless, or orphans.

Below are some sample target groups. Circle all of the ones that apply to you, and then choose the one that most appropriately describes who you feel you are called to serve, be around, and inspire. The words below are examples only, to help you. If your target group is not in this list, feel free to add it.

Abused   Actors   Adults   Animal(s)   Businessmen
Children   Deaf   Discouraged   Divorced   Dying   Elderly
Ethnic Group   Grieving   Handicapped   Homeless
Impoverished   Lonely   Men   Musicians   Newly married
Non-believers   Orphans   People in general   Politicians
Race of people   Singers   Singles   Teachers   Teens
Women   Writers   _____   _____

MY TARGET GROUP:

_____

(the group/cause which most moves/excites you)

My Mission Statement

(Finished Statement)

_____
(Your Name)

My mission Is To:

_____, _____, and _____
(Your three primary passions - your three action verbs)

_____
(Your underlying value - your one noun)

in, to, for, with or through
(circle the appropriate word above)

_____
(the group/cause which most moves/excites you)

How To Use Your Mission Statement

1. Memorize Your Mission

Make your mission one of your primary thoughts. Repeat your mission statement over and over again, until you have it memorized. Become so familiar with it, that you are able to recall it, even without thought.

2. Meditate On Your Mission

Look at your mission. Each time you look at it, focus on a different word, and reflect on that word. Declare to yourself what that word means, and why it is so important to you.

Or, rewrite your mission on a sheet of paper five times, once for each Primary Passion, once for your Underlying Value, and once for your Target Group. Each time capitalize a different word. Reflect on each word.

3. Pray Your Mission

Let your mission become your focus for the day. Every day, when you get up, pray your mission. Ask God to help you in that day, to fulfill your mission. Commit your day to God, to fulfill your mission. Ask God for opportunities to be active in your mission.

4. Evaluate Your Previous Week's Success

Write down all of your activities during the last seven days. Then evaluate how each one of your activities helped you to fulfill your mission, or bring you closer to your mission. Are there activities you need to drop, add, or fine-tune, in order to become more focused on your mission?

5. Quiz People On Your Mission

Ask people who know you, to guess what your mission is, based on how they observe your words and activities. Are you effectively speaking, demonstrating, and living your mission?

6. Share Your Mission

Write your mission in large letters on a white board, or a flip chart or other large piece of paper or cardboard, and encourage your workmates, friends or family to give you feedback on how they feel you are accomplishing your mission.

7. Enlist Personal Feedback On Your Mission

When having a coffee or meal with someone who knows you, write your mission statement on a napkin or paper placemat, and ask them to share what your mission means to them. Then ask them if they see that mission being expressed in you.

8. Create A Short Devotional Based On Your Mission

Create a short, five to seven minute devotional based on your mission, including an appropriate biblical text and a few key points. Then, share that devotional with a few people with whom you are in relationship, to whom you are accountable, and ask for their feedback.

9. Evaluate Your Planning Process

Sit down and evaluate your planning process, and how you use your mission statement in your daily, weekly, and monthly planning.

10. Find Role Models Who Live Your Mission

Write down the names of five people who have a mission very similar to yours, and discover what steps they have taken to fulfill their mission. You may need to have a short meeting with them, in person or on the phone, or you may need to read their biography.

11. Have Others Describe Their Concept Of Your Mission

Have a few people who know you, write a mission statement for you, based on their perception of your activities and focus. Does their perceived mission of you agree with your mission? Why or why not? How can your mission become more obvious to others?

The Goal: Fruitfulness In Your Mission

If you do the above assignments, and others like them, they will help you to focus your life on your mission, and become more effective in your mission. And that is the goal; fruitfulness in your life's mission.

The Need For A Couple's Mission Statement

Over the years I have come to believe that although the greatest cause of marriage conflict is lack of communication, one of the other causes near the top is a lack of "Couple's Mission".

What I mean by that, is that most people have never discovered what their mission in life is, and so they cannot communicate it to their future spouse. Then, after marriage, each person begins to discover their mission, and to their surprise, they find out:

Their mission is incompatible with their spouse's mission, or their mission is in some degree conflicting or divergent from their spouse's mission.

This leads to conflicting emotions, conflicting schedules, conflicting focus, conflicting values, conflicting priorities, conflicting paths, and just plain conflict.

Amos 3:3, NLT – *(3) Can two people walk together without agreeing on the direction?*

Certainly, every person is unique in so many ways, but unless there is some common sense of mission, in at least a part of their life, their lives will slowly drift apart.

When I was a (much) younger man, I took a city bus ride in Peterborough, Ontario. I sat beside a woman who appeared to be in her mid-thirties, and was looking rather depressed. I felt to begin a conversation with her, with the goal of sharing the love of Jesus with her. Within minutes she said, "Oh, I know all about Christianity – I used to be a Christian". At that point, my goal of turning her heart to Christ became the goal of understanding her heart. So I asked her if she would share her story.

She shared that she had become a Christian in her late teens, and began to attend a very good church in the city. She loved children, and so became very active in the large church nursery, as well as in the preschool class. A few years later she met a young man who loved people, especially the poor and struggling, and the homeless. She was so impressed the way that he would walk down the street, and see a struggling person or a homeless person, and immediately go out of his way to demonstrate his love and compassion for them. Because her own father was somewhat harsh and distant, she was magnetically drawn to his warmth and compassion.

At the same time, he was drawn by her pure and sincere mother's heart, so gentle, so tender, and so loving toward the children, and he just knew that he wanted to marry someone who would be such a great mother.

So the two were soon married, excited to begin their life of mutual love and compassion together. After they returned from their one-week honeymoon, they looked forward to serving Christ together as committed Christians.

A day or two later, she woke up in the morning to discover a strange, old man sleeping on their couch, and smelling up the main floor of their house. She quickly ran to her new husband, and said "who is that strange man on our coach?" He responded, "Dear, you know how much I love the poor and struggling and homeless, and I met this man on the street last night, let him use our shower, and gave him the new pajamas to wear that you bought me while I washed his clothes. I knew that you wouldn't mind." Although she did mind, especially since the man was wearing the pajamas that she had bought especially for him, but she tried not to show her frustration (or her fear for her safety, because she did not know if this strange man was safe).

A few nights later, she awoke in the morning to find a strange woman sleeping on their couch, wearing her brand new night gown. Again, she ran to her husband, only to be told: "Dear, you know how much I love the poor and struggling and homeless, and I met this woman on the street last night, let her use our shower, and gave her your new nightgown to wear. By the way, her clothes were all frayed and worn, so I gave her some of your clothes to wear. I knew that you would mind." Again, she tried to hide her fear and frustration, but this time it lasted several days.

Sadly, this same scenario happened week in and week about, and within about six months, sadly, they were divorced. She said that there was no way she could stay married to man who would not provide a safe environment for their (soon to come) children. He said that there was no way he could stay married to a woman who would not allow him to obey God's call on his life.

How could a Christian couple who loved Christ and loved each other divorce? Because they did not have a common mission. His mission was to reach the poor and struggling and homeless, and that required a very secure and sacrificial and hospitable spouse. However, her mission was to care for babies and young children, and this requires a very safe and secure environment, and a husband who would create and maintain a safe home environment at all costs. Their missions just did not converge, and so they could not walk together.

The following pages are designed to help you develop a "Couple's Mission" Statement that you can develop and use to keep your marriage walking in the same direction.

Couple's Mission Statement Worksheet

1. Couple's Primary Passions (Verbs)

In the left column, write down the husband's "Seven Verbs Which Inspire Me" that he selected in Section 2. In the right column, write down the wife's "Seven Verbs Which Inspire Me" that she selected in Section 2.

Husband	Wife
_____	_____
_____	_____
_____	_____
_____	_____
_____	_____
_____	_____
_____	_____

Now choose three verbs that together, as a couple, you can agree are most like the two of you as a couple.

_____   _____

_____

2. Couple's Underlying Values (Nouns)

In the left column, write down the husband's "Three Nouns Which Inspire Me" that he selected in Section 2. In the right column, write down the wife's "Three Nouns Which Inspire Me" that she selected in Section 2.

Husband	Wife
_____	_____
_____	_____
_____	_____

Now choose the one noun that together, as a couple, you can agree is most like the two of you as a couple.

_____

3. Couple's Target Group

From all of the target groups that the two of you circled in Section 2, choose the one target group that the two of you together can agree on, that you would like to serve as a couple.

Our Target Group:

_____

(the group/cause which most moves/excites us as a couple)

4. Couple's Mission Statement

Take your agreed upon Primary Passions (verbs) and Underlying Values (nouns) and target group, and put them into the blanks below.

Then, using the skills learned in the "Strengthening Your Mission Statement", refine you Couple's Mission Statement until it really resonates in both your hearts.

(Note: If you cannot build a couple's mission statement using your seven verbs and three nouns, go back to your twelve verbs and ten nouns, and try again).

Our Mission Statement

(Finished Statement)

_____ and _____
(Your Names)

Our mission Is To:

_____, _____, and _____
(Your three primary passions - your three action verbs)

_____
(Your underlying value - your one noun)

in, to, for, with or through
(circle the appropriate word above)

_____
(the group/cause which most moves/excites you)

5. Embrace And Apply Your Couple's Mission Statement

a) Refine

Take time as a couple to discuss your couple's mission statement. Refine it as much as you need to, until you both feel a real agreement and excitement about it.

b) Brainstorm

Now, take time as a couple to brainstorm ideas of how you can express this mission statement as a couple. What things do you need to investigate? Where do you need to volunteer? What do you need to try? It make take several attempts together, but you will find the perfect place where the two of you can serve together.

c) Apply

Now, step out. Make a commitment to serve together, in your church, on your street, in your community, with a social agency, wherever you feel you can best express your mission together.

d) Have Fun

Try! Explore! Serve! Evaluate! Have Fun!

Our Mission Statement

(Finished Statement)

_____ and _____
(Your Names)

Our mission Is To:

_____, _____, and _____
(Your three primary passions - your three action verbs)

_____
(Your underlying value - your one noun)

in, to, for, with or through
(circle the appropriate word above)

_____
(the group/cause which most moves/excites you)

Appendices

How To Begin Your Journey With God

John 14:6, NIV - *Jesus answered, "I am the way and the truth and the life. No one comes to the Father except through me.*

Living a life in partnership with God, through His Son Jesus, is the greatest adventure any person can ever experience. How can we make the initial decision to trust Him with our whole life, and begin to live for Him? It's as easy as A-B-C-D!

A – Admit that Jesus is indeed the only way to salvation, and that our hearts are completely lost without Him. (Romans 3:23, Romans 3:10).

B – Believe that Jesus died on the cross for our sins, and rose from the dead for our freedom. (John 1:29, John 3:16-18, Acts 4:12).

C – Confess Jesus as our personal Lord and Saviour, the new leader of our lives. (Romans 10:9, John 5:24, John 1:12-13).

D – Decide to follow Jesus daily, and do what He asks of us. (Luke 9:23-24).

PRAYER

We can make those four choices, by saying a prayer something like this:

Jesus, I realize that I am lost without You, and You are the only way that I can experience freedom.

Thank You for dying on the cross to save me from the penalty of sin, and for rising from the dead so that I could be completely free.

I choose to confess and put my trust in You as my Lord and Savior. I give my whole heart and my whole life to You.

I ask You to indwell me by Your Holy Spirit, so that I can have Your help to do my best to follow You and please You each and every day.

In Jesus' name I pray. Amen!

Who Is David R. Hibbert?

David R. Hibbert grew up on the edge of a farm in rural Ontario, just north of London. After graduating from the University of Western Ontario, he worked as an Electrical-Mechanical Maintenance and Design Engineer in Hamilton, Ontario, before accepting the call to full-time Christian ministry.

During Bible school training in Peterborough, Ontario, he spent his summers as an interim Pastor in Northern Ontario. Upon graduation, he served as the Director of a Men's Mission for two years.

Then, at the leading of the Holy Spirit, he moved to the South Shore of Montreal, Quebec, Canada to plant a church and develop an Apostolic Centre.

He enjoys teaching, exhortation, short-term missions and developing training courses, books, and manuals. His Mission Statement is "to build, equip, and release purpose in people's lives."

He is married to an incredible woman named Kathleen, and has four grown awesome children – Kristen, Thomas, Kaylea and Elissa – as well as a growing number of grandchildren.

Other Books And Courses By David R. Hibbert

Note: These books are available around the world as paperbacks through Amazon, and as eBooks through Amazon and www.DestinyResource.ca.

Answering The BIG Questions

Every few years it is good to check our foundations, to see if there are any cracks in them, or if they have shifted because of the pressures of life.

"Answering The BIG Questions" is a new and fresh look at the really BIG questions of life, to ensure that our lives are still built on a good foundation. We look at God's Original Purpose, Understanding What We Lost, Understanding What We Really Need, Understanding How The Spirit Conforms Us, Understanding Our New Identity, and Understanding How To Live in Victory. A refreshing and liberating study of how to live as a child of God.

Building An Apostolic Centre

In this book we will develop an understanding of what an Apostolic Centre is, how the early church grew because of Apostolic Centres, and what are the basic ingredients that are necessary to ensure the establishment of a healthy Apostolic Centre that will bless the region and advance the Kingdom of God within that region.

Christmas Quizzicles

This eBook is a collection of some quizzes, games, stories, and inspirational notes – some serious, some thought-provoking, and some just plain silly. They are just a sampling of the many that I've collected over the years ... fun resources for children of all ages. May you enjoy them as much I have enjoyed collecting them.

These quizzes are great for family gatherings, small groups, church parties and more. Simply copy, hand out, and let the fun begin. Now have fun and celebrate!

Developing An Intentional Culture For Your Church, Business Or Family – Determining Your Relational Atmosphere

A culture is the relational atmosphere that every organization must have, in order to be healthy and effective. In this book David Hibbert explains the critical importance of planning, documenting, and promoting the desired culture. Although this book is written primarily for church communities, it applies equally as well to any group where people must work and co-exist together.

Discovering Your P.U.R.P.O.S.E.: Volume I – Developing A Personal Mission Statement

You have a purpose, a destiny, a special assignment from God Himself! And when you discover that purpose, commit to that purpose, and make decisions in alignment with that purpose, the Creator of the universe ensures that all of the resources in heaven and earth are directed toward you, so that you can fulfill that purpose.

There are seven primary indicators that God has given you, to help you discover what is your purpose in life. In Volume One of "Discovering Your P.U.R.P.O.S.E.", you will be taught the first two indicators to discover what is your purpose, and then be guided, step by step, to developing your own personal Mission Statement for your life, that you can use to help you stay on track, and make the best decisions for your life's purpose.

This Book can change the direction and focus of your life!

Discovering Your P.U.R.P.O.S.E.: Volume II – Realizing Your Specific Assignment

You have a purpose, a destiny, a special assignment from God Himself! And when you discover that purpose, commit to that purpose, and make decisions in alignment with that purpose, the Creator of the universe ensures that all of the resources in heaven and earth are directed toward you, so that you can fulfill that purpose.

There are seven primary indicators that God has given you, to help you discover what is your purpose in life. In Volume Two of "Discovering Your P.U.R.P.O.S.E.", you will discover your Reoccurring Experiences,

Personality Traits, Overriding Motivations, Spiritual Gifts and Extra
Resources that you have, that will help you to fine-tune your purpose into
a specific area of God-given assignment.

This Book can change the direction and focus of your life!

Embracing The Fivefold Ministry – Volume I – Introduction To The Fivefold Ministry

In this introduction to the fivefold ministry, you will discover the purpose of
the fivefold ministries, their differences, how they work together in a
church service, what happens when a church is only one-fold or two-fold,
and church government in a fivefold church.

Embracing The Fivefold Ministry – Volume II – Understanding The Apostolic Ministry

Coming soon!

Embracing The Fivefold Ministry – Volume III – Understanding The Prophetic Ministry

Coming soon!

Experience Resurrection Power: By Embracing The Cross

In this Book, David Hibbert looks at the three parts of the cross; the
vertical board, the horizontal board, and the foot of the cross, to explain
the three most important things that Jesus did on the cross for us. He
also shares a little understood consequence of Jesus' work on the cross
that is indispensable to embrace, if we are going to truly experience
Christian maturity in our lives. He clearly describes what must happen
when we come to the cross if we want resurrection power in our lives. He
also shares an amazing fact about an overlooked Christian ordinance
that was designed by God to give us a special impartation of grace for
experiencing resurrection power.

Fasting Made (Super) Simple

Biblical fasting has been very much misunderstood by many, if not most
people. Because of that, for those who have tried to fast, and seen

minimal or no results, it has left a poor impression on them. In this eBook you will be given very simple step-by-step and practical information on how anyone can fast, as well as the hidden key to fasting that will unlock its power for your life. Get ready for breakthrough!

F.E.A.R.L.E.S.S. – Eight Keys To Overcoming Fear

Fear is one of humankind's greatest enemies. At the least, it hinders and limits us. At the most, it keeps us in bondage, and plays havoc on our health, our relationships, and our potential. In this book David Hibbert gives you 8 keys to help you overcome every fear in your life.

Feasting On Christ's Grace At His Table

God has lovingly provided for His children, many sources of His amazing grace. Come and understand, and receive, the incredible grace of God that is available to each one of us, when we recognize it, and learn how to receive it, through the celebration of the Lord's Supper, also known as the Lord's Table, or Communion.

Five Keys For Effective Prayer Evangelism

In this book, David Hibbert shares with the reader five rarely used keys for praying for those who do not yet know Christ, or who have wandered away from faith in Christ. The task of bringing people to Christ is not just about preaching the gospel, it is also about waging spiritual warfare against Satan's tactics that affect a person's mind and heart and spiritual sight. Apply these five Biblical keys, and see your prayer effectiveness reach a whole new level!

Forgiveness – The Key To Freedom

Forgiveness is such a really big deal! So many people struggle with unforgiveness, resentment, and personal wounds caused by others. And it is keeping so many people sick, limited, bound up, and side-tracked. God wants us to be free. Jesus died so that we can be free. But until we learn how to forgive, and live a life of forgiveness towards others, we will never be free.

This book looks at the topic of forgiveness … what it is, what is isn't, why is it difficult to forgive, why we need to forgive, Biblical mindsets that help us forgive, and how we can truly forgive, so that we can be completely free in our lives.

Healing Father Wounds

Most Christians today have so much knowledge about Jesus, and yet we tend to be ineffective and unproductive. Why is this so? Because we are lacking certain qualities in our lives, because of father wounds. So we need to have our father wounds healed, so that our knowledge can be translated into effectiveness.

In this book, you will discover what father wounds are, how you received your father wounds, how they affect your life, and God's amazing plan to re-parent you, so that you can be healed from all of your father wounds, and become the effective son or daughter of God that you were created to be.

Healing It's Yours

In this book David Hibbert uses much Biblical support to tackle the question, "It is always God's will to heal?" He then challenges us to consider that we may the solution to our own healing. Next he presents many practical scriptures and examples to understand both keys to healing, and how to keep your healing. A very practical and Biblical explanation of healing for today.

How To Experience True Freedom

God wants us to become truly free. He wants us to experience the fullness of His forgiveness today, and He wants us to be free so that we do not repeat the cycle of failure in our lives.

This book will give you the understanding and tools you need to experience true freedom in your life. Experience true freedom from all guilt and shame and remorse, as well as damaged emotions from the offenses of others.

How To Gather Purposefully

When Christians meet together on a Sunday, why are they meeting? What is their goal? What do they expect to accomplish? Does God have any expectations from them?

This message will help Christians to understand how to meet with purpose and intention, so that God is truly glorified, His will is accomplished, and people are blessed by God as they meet. This message is very encouraging, practical, and brings much clarity to the gather of the local church.

How To Have A Healing Ministry

God wants every believer in Christ to share the love of Christ, minister to those who are suffering, and invite people into the Kingdom of God. The ministry of healing is a powerful tool to open hearts to the gospel. In this teaching, David Hibbert details ten keys that are necessary for anyone wanting to have a sustainable healing ministry. He also shares a proven ten step checklist for connecting with the sick, receiving permission to pray for them, and maximizing healing results. Very insightful, practical, and challenging.

How To Hear God's Voice – Five Keys For Clarity

Every Christian wants to know God's will, but to know the fullness of God's will, we need to be able to hear His voice.

In this book, you will be given a simple, yet very effective strategy for hearing God's voice. You will be amazed at how easy it is for you to hear God's voice. And you will be motivated to begin a life-long journey in daily hearing His voice and live in a new level of effectiveness in your walk with God.

How To Intercede For Your City

If we are a Christian, each one of us has a divine mandate to bring the gospel to our city. But we are often unsure what to do, how to do it, and how to be effective in doing it.

In this book you will learn how to intercede for your city, in a way, that you will actually see some results. This book is very practical, and includes information on the Biblical definition of nations, recent data on unreached and unengaged people groups, and statistics on migration from rural to city.

How To Self-Publish An eBook In Canada

For all of the aspiring authors out there, here is a very clear and simple explanation of the steps necessary to self-publish an eBook in Canada. Included in this book is information on the types, categories and main formats of eBooks, guidance on how to write an eBook, obtaining an ISBN number, opening an Amazon Kindle Direct Publishing Account, preparing, and publishing your eBook, and more.

Keys To Intimacy – Experiencing The Heart Of God

There is no trust without intimacy. Intimacy builds trust. In this series you will learn eight simple keys that will enable you to deepen your relationship with the lover of your soul and come to trust Him in a whole new way.

Learning How To Love: Manifesting Agape

Most of us still experience conflicts and offenses and damaged relationships. If love truly is as powerful a force as we say it is, then we must be willing to ask a very serious question: "Do we really know how to love?" This book examines the different types of love, gives a thorough description of the highest form of love, and then presents simple strategies to develop the skills necessary to express this amazing love – God's love.

Making The Most Of The Christmas Season: Inspiration For A Great Christmas And An Awesome New Year

Christmas can be a CRAZY time. Planning for family gatherings, getting presents for those we love, reconnecting with friends, navigating through Christmas and Boxing Day (now boxing week) sales, and not to mention the dreaded "year end" inventory lists and financial statements. What on earth happened to "Merry Christmas and a Happy New Year"?

In this book, the reader will be presented with five strategies to make Christmas both meaningful and enjoyable, and be able to face the New Year with hope and expectation. In all, these five strategic attitudes are easily implemented, and can make the difference between year-end panic, and year end hope for an even better year ahead.

Natural Discipleship

We are first and foremost children of God, and we become children of God the moment we become a Christian, and we are immediately placed into the family of God. So what if our growth to maturity is not agreement to a list of doctrinal statements, and a development of good Christian habits? What if our spiritual growth as Christians actually follows the same process as the natural growth of children into adulthood.

This book will show you how the best way to mature in Christ, is to follow the same five steps as natural growth of every child into adulthood.

No Fear – Choose Peace And Grow Stronger In A Time Of Crisis

In this book, published during the COVID-19 pandemic of 2020, David Hibbert presents a Christian perspective on crisis, and then shares a number of important principles on how to face a crisis as a Christian, including how to do spiritual warfare during a crisis, how to pursue and fulfill your God-given purpose during a crisis, how to grow spiritually during a time of crisis, and how to stay in the peace of God during a crisis. This book will give you very practical tools so that you can go through the storm, and come out even stronger.

Overcoming Fear In A Time Of Crisis – 28 Truths To Exchange Fear For Peace

This book was birthed in the middle of the COVID-19 pandemic of 2020, but the truths in it can equally apply to any pandemic or crisis in our lives. God's Word is applicable to every situation, and so this book will help you whether you are facing another world-wide epidemic, or a more focused personal crisis.

Read each chapter, consider it, meditate on it, and be encouraged. God is with you in your storm, and He will bring you to the other side!

Overcoming Self-Deception

When I first became a Christian, it seemed like everyone I met was concerned about doctrinal error. Do we believe the right things about the doctrine of the Holy Spirit, do we believe the right things about salvation, do we believe the right things about Jesus, do we believe the right things about the end times? In those early days, most error seemed to revolve around our interpretation of the scriptures. Today, however, much of the error that I have come across isn't due to our interpretation of the scriptures, but due to our philosophy of how we even approach the Scriptures.

In this short book, I will look at what I believe is one of the most widespread errors in the church today, and then present a principle that will bring balance back to this error, as well as serve as a tool to avoid other errors in the future.

Overcoming The Orphan Stronghold

We believe that every Christian wants to be "fully conformed to the image of Christ" – they want to become all that they were created to be, and to fulfill their destiny here on earth.

However, every person on earth, including Christians, struggles with the orphan stronghold. It affects our faith in God, our ability to trust God, our ability to trust people, our ability to relate with others, our ability to have healthy marriages, our freedom in Christ, our healing, and even our destiny.

In these lessons, you will learn what the Orphan Stronghold is, where it came from, how it operates, how it manifests in us, and how we can begin to overcome it. God wants us free to be fully alive in Him!

Receiving The Seven-Fold Spirit Of God

In this book you will discover why most people, including many in the Pentecostal and Charismatic theological streams, have missed the full benefits of Pentecost. You will also discover what is the Seven-Fold Spirit of God, and how to embrace the fullness of the Holy Spirit. Get ready for breakthrough!

Seven Keys To Maturity In Christ

Most Christians want to grow in Christ, and to become mature Christians. But how is that accomplished? In this book we present seven keys that you can use to jump-start, and even quicken your Christian growth, as well as guarantee continued growth for the rest of your life. Learn how to apply the Keys of Liberty, Conformity, Identity, Authority, Clarity, Community, and Intimacy and discover the joy of maturity in Christ.

The Blessing Of Personal Prophecy

In this book, David Hibbert defines prophecy, public prophecy, and personal prophecy, and then validates Biblically that God uses people to minister personal prophecy today. Finally he gives very practical guidelines for receiving, understanding, and responding to a personal prophetic word.

This book will answer the questions: What is Prophecy? Is Prophecy Still Valid Today? What Is The Purpose Of Prophecy? Our Response To Prophecy. How To Maximize The Blessing Of Your Prophecy. What Should Be Our Response To Prophecy? How To Maximize The Blessing Of Your Prophecy.

The Four Pillars Of Christian Maturity

In this book, David Hibbert looks at the Four Pillars Of Christian Maturity, as outlined in Acts 2:42-47. He explains each of the four pillars, and then gives practical examples of why they are so important to our spiritual health and maturity. He also gives a graphic example of what will happen to our spiritual life if we neglect these four pillars.

The Power of a Blessing

Every human being longs for love, longs for acceptance, longs for the knowledge that they are valued by someone, and that they have a purpose worth living for. God has given us the principle of blessing as a way to deposit within a person's heart, the assurance of all of these things. Learn how to transform a person's life for greatness, with your words and actions, in this simple five-part Biblical principle.

The Search For A Father: The Story Of David

In this insightful book, you will experience an intimate examination of David's search for a father, from his infancy, as a teen, and into his adult years. You will discover the cause of much of his failure, the source of much of his pain, and the secret of his later years of success. And you will conclude that he found what we all need, the presence of a godly father.

When Christians Face Crises

Why did this happen? Why did God allow it? Does God really care? These are some of the many questions that are asked "When Christians Face Crises". This book is not about religious platitudes are simplistic arguments. Instead, the writer seeks to give clear, Biblical answers to our very difficult questions concerning pain and suffering. This book will give the reader a compassionate and Biblical perspective on suffering and inspire hope to those presently in the midst of a crisis.

End Notes

[1] The Dash Poem, ©1996 Linda Ellis, http://lindaellis.net/
[2] http://go.roberts.edu/leadingedge/the-great-choices-of-strategic-leaders
[3] http://bradblackman.com/rut/
[4] http://www.azquotes.com/quote/856466
[5] Matthew 5:14
[6] Esther 4:14
[7] Romans 8:29-30; Ephesians 1:5, 11
[8] Ephesians 2:10
[9] Revelation 21:2
[10] John 5:35; 15:16
[11] John 15:5,8
[12] Philippians 1:6
[13] Ephesians 3:16,20; 2 Timothy 1:7; 2 Thessalonians 1:11; Colossians 1:11
[14] https://www.youtube.com/watch?v=QrbUuLt05wg
[15] https://www.youtube.com/watch?v=7gVCJ5l0VH0
[16] https://www.brainyquote.com/quotes/quotes/m/mothertere158110.html
[17] https://www.brainyquote.com/quotes/quotes/m/mothertere131834.html
[18] https://www.brainyquote.com/quotes/quotes/m/mothertere130839.html
[19] https://www.brainyquote.com/quotes/quotes/m/mothertere105649.html
[20] https://www.brainyquote.com/quotes/quotes/m/mothertere158105.html
[21] https://www.brainyquote.com/quotes/quotes/b/billygraha626324.html
[22] https://www.brainyquote.com/quotes/quotes/b/billygraha150661.html
[23] http://www.azquotes.com/quote/1450532
[24] http://zedekiahlist.com/cgi-bin/quotes.pl?&id=32852476
[25] http://listverse.com/2011/09/30/top-10-strong-human-fears/
[26] https://tifwe.org/fear-of-a-meaningless-life/
[27] https://www.theguardian.com/technology/2016/nov/27/genevieve-bell-ai-robotics-anthropologist-robots
[28] Laurie Beth Jones, "The Path: Creating Your Mission Statement for Work and for Life", Hachette Books; Reprint edition (Aug. 19 1998)

Made in the USA
Columbia, SC
04 September 2021

44917599R00086